Manspeak

Manspeak

What He Says and What He Really Means

by Marnie Winston-Macauley

Andrews and McMeel
A Universal Press Syndicate Company
Kansas City

ISBN: 0-8362-2225-3
Library of Congress Catalog Card Number: 96-84527

CONTENTS

ACKNOWLEDGMENTS

To the Truthspeakers: As always, there's my guiding guru and dear colleague, Alan Garner. Then, the dynamic team at Andrews and McMeel (and Universal Press): Tom Thornton, Dorothy O'Brien, Michael Nonbello, Eden Blackwood, Allan Stark, Nancy Meis, Polly Blair, and of course, Hugh Andrews. A very special thanks to Barr Seitz, my producer at ABC Love Online, who spirited me into cyberspace and has been both my left and right hands. To my personal "yay-sayers" who simply BELIEVE that something in creative craziness "speaketh the truth"—and support that journey. They are: Dr. Joshua and Jill Winston, Terry Lester, Craig Kelso, Stephanie Winston, Rita Lloyd, Charles and Mary Keating, Marta Sanders, Julie Poll, Allyson Rice-Taylor, Laurence and Pat Caso, Dr. Robert U. Akeret, Dr. Albert Stanek, and John H. Johnson. And love, too, to "the family" in New York, Toronto, Missouri, West Virginia, Florida, and Wales.

And of course . . . to "the source"—my husband, Ian.

DEDICATION:

To all those who provided me (alas) with firsthand experience in the art and "craft"-iness of "Manspeak." They include (but are not limited to):

Howie . . . my third-grade boyfriend, whose nails I buffed so he'd pass hygiene inspection—and who passed me a note the last day of class, saying, "I meant what I said in gym about loving you always, Kim."

All the "swingle" guys in the sixties at Maxwell's Plum who wrote my number on matchbook covers and swore we'd catch a Grand Funk concert "next Saturday." I'm still waiting.

Jesse . . . the "actor"-waiter in the Borscht Belt whose lessons (and nose-job) I financed in 1975—who still won't throw in an extra pickle when he serves me at Deli King.

Every lawyer, agent, and network executive (male and female)—for elevating Manspeak to a wildly successful linguistic alternative.

But most of all to my son, Simon, who after reading this book will know the difference between Manspeak and Truthspeak . . . and will put Mommy out of business.

—*Marnie*

INTRODUCTION

Why can't men and women communicate? Choose one.
- A) We're smarter.
- B) We're more honest.
- C) We're able to speak our native language.
- D) We're not genetically defective.
- E) All of the above.

If you chose "All of the Above," you may actually have a shot at a two-line chat with a member of the male species without courting a nervous breakdown.

For starters, realize that while there are some males out there who are indeed, lying swine, most actually believe (more or less) what they're saying. They suffer, however, from a sex-related language disorder, called "Manspeak." Since Manspeak, which consists of up to two short grunts, comes from the lower half of their bodies, most men aren't aware that what comes out of their mouths has little or no connection to their brains.

INTRODUCTION

Now, to crack the "Manspeak" code, you can either:

1) Spend thirty years studying the species—and wind up ranting their strange mumblings like, "Me want nookie," as they wheel you away to a padded room.

2) Spend your days (and nights) complaining to your therapist, your mother, and the lady who spritzes perfume on you at the mall…"But he *said/ promised/ swore, he would:* _____ (FILL IN THE BLANK) *love me only, remember our anniversary THIS year, finish painting the ceiling, put the toilet seat down, have a vasectomy.*"

3) Spend your life on the planet "unmanned." However, blissful as this may sound, they DO have a vital part or two that makes coupling more fun than quilting comforters or reading *Moby Dick* to your cats. (Usually.)

– OR –

4) Read on and learn how to decipher **What He Says…and What He *Really* Means!**

_____

Is It an Artichoke...Or Is It a Man?

HE SAYS: "How can you say I don't care about your birthday?"

HE MEANS: "Didn't I buy you a *Buns of Steel* tape?"

1

HE SAYS: "Of **course** I'm listening to you."

HE *MEANS*:   "Should I get a lube job or just go for a car wash tomorrow?"

· ·

HE SAYS: "You know I'm interested in your feelings."

HE *MEANS*:   "When you *feel* like sex or getting me a beer."

HE SAYS: "I'm giving you cash for Christmas this year, darling, because I want you to be happy and get exactly what you want."

HE MEANS: "And so I don't have to get within twenty feet of a store—or make a decision."

HE SAYS: "It's a damn shame you and your family aren't speaking."

HE **MEANS**: "Yes! Ten-dollar phone bills!"

· ·

HE SAYS: "You deserve to be treated like royalty."

HE **MEANS**: "I'm taking you to the Dairy Queen."

HE SAYS: (In your new $500 gown) "Yeah…you look fine, babe."

HE **MEANS**: "Did you change…?"

. . . .

HE SAYS: "Your poem? Hey…I keep it right by my bedside."

HE **MEANS**: "Under the pizza box in the waste-paper basket."

HE SAYS: (After you've dyed your hair blonde) "Of course I see a difference."

HE **MEANS**: "Could it be a nose job...or an artificial leg...?"

....

HE SAYS: "I try to be a sensitive husband."

HE **MEANS**: "I try not to call out my girlfriend's name when I'm in bed with my wife."

HE SAYS: "Sure I appreciate the hours you spent on this mushroom soufflé with truffles."

HE **MEANS**: "But I'd appreciate a bottle of ketchup a hell of a lot more!"

· ·

HE SAYS: (When you've been running a 104-degree fever, while doubled over in pain and shivering under the blankets for three days) "Hey…everything okay, babe?"

HE **MEANS**: "If I ignore it, maybe she'll have sex—since she's in bed anyway."

HE SAYS: "My eyes are closed because I'm concentrating on finding a solution to your problem."

HE **MEANS**: "Wake me when you're done."

. . . .

HE SAYS: "Of course I missed you while you were away."

HE **MEANS**: "You were away...?"

———

HE SAYS: "I want to learn everything there is to know about you."

HE MEANS: "If you can keep it to under thirty seconds."

Close Encounters of the Strangest Kind: Dating & Mating

HE *SAYS*:   "I can't remember when I felt this way about a woman."

HE *MEANS*:   "Was it **two** or **three** nights ago in the Pussycat Lounge?"

HE SAYS: "I've got **you**, babe, so who needs to go out?"

HE MEANS: "I've got a bed and a six-pack, so why blow money on dinner?"

HE SAYS: "Sure, I'll take you to a restaurant with entertainment."

HE **MEANS**: "A wide-screen TV tuned to a hockey game."

....

HE SAYS: "Can I give you a lift home...?"

HE **MEANS**: "Can I give you a lift to MY home."

HE SAYS: " I am not 'just' using you."

HE **MEANS**: "I'm using five other broads as well!"

· ·

HE SAYS: "I consider that privileged information."

HE **MEANS**: "My name, my address, my home phone, my occupation, and my marital status."

HE SAYS: "Don't worry, I'll pick you up at 8 P.M. sharp on Valentine's Day."

HE **MEANS**: "That's sometime in May, right?"

. . . .

HE SAYS: "I have so many important things on my mind, how can I be expected to remember the little things?"

HE **MEANS**: "Like your birthday or the fact that I'm married and have five kids."

HE SAYS: "I haven't found the right woman."

HE **MEANS**: "I have, however, **lost** 250 of them."

· ·

HE SAYS: "I'm really flattered you want to have my children."

HE **MEANS**: "If I get a running start, I can make it to the Mexican border by midnight."

HE SAYS: "I want us to develop a meaningful relationship."

HE **MEANS**: "I want to make it with you."

....

HE SAYS: "What do you mean I'm not romantic?"

HE **MEANS**: "Don't I hold your hand during halftime?"

HE SAYS: "I believe in practicing safe sex."

HE **MEANS**: "I only fool around when my wife is out of town."

· ·

HE SAYS: "I don't usually relate to women this easily."

HE **MEANS**: "I don't usually score this easily."

HE S<small>AYS</small>: "I call you 'babe' because you're special to me."

HE **M**EANS: "...and because I forgot your name."

· ·

HE S<small>AYS</small>: "I'm into foreign films."

HE **M**EANS: *Emmanuel, More Emmanuel,* and *The Best of Emmanuel.*"

HE SAYS: "Looks aren't everything."

HE **MEANS**: "In the dark—and if you put out."

· ·

HE SAYS: "Unlike some jerks, I pride myself on giving a woman all the foreplay she needs."

HE **MEANS**: "As much as three whole minutes!"

HE SAYS: "Yes, I'm 'available.'"

HE **MEANS**: "For a one-night stand in Vegas."

· ·

HE SAYS: "I'm looking for a woman who is easy to be with."

HE **MEANS**: "I'm looking for a woman who is 'easy.'"

HE SAYS: "I'm good with my hands."

HE **MEANS**: "I can unhook a Wonderbra in under five seconds."

· ·

HE SAYS: "I'm alone too."

HE **MEANS**: "My date's in the john."

HE SAYS: "It was special for me too, babe."

HE **MEANS**: "If I hurry, I can make it to the singles bar by three."

. . . .

HE SAYS: "I'd like to see more of you."

HE **MEANS**: "Your tits, for starters."

HE SAYS: "My idea of a perfect blind date is a girl meeting me at the door, with an apron on."

HE **MEANS**: "And nothing underneath except cellophane."

HE SAYS: "Tell me...was it terrific for you, or what?"

HE **MEANS**: "Tell me, was **I** terrific, or what!"

· ·

HE SAYS: "Of course I want more than a one-night stand, babe."

HE **MEANS**: "Nooners are good, too."

———

Personal Ads: Creative Writing 101

HE *WRITES*: "Autumn male seeks female to make him feel like Spring again."

HE *MEANS*: "Old fart wants young action."

HE *WRITES*: "Likes simple unpretentious life."

HE **MEANS**: "It's strictly bologna and beer, babe."

· ·

HE *WRITES*: "Personable."

HE **MEANS**: "I look like Godzilla—but I'm friendly."

HE *WRITES*: "Seeking financially secure woman."

HE **MEANS**: "I went to the Kato Kaelin school of employment."

· ·

HE *WRITES*: "A small medical problem shouldn't keep soulmates apart."

HE **MEANS**: "I'm on life support."

HE *WRITES*: "Seeks open-minded woman with style."

HE **MEANS**: "Seeks woman who will let me wear her stilettos and bustier on alternate Saturday nights."

· ·

HE *WRITES*: "Wanted! Gal-meister for wild and crazy fun-meister!"

HE **MEANS**: "I wear white socks, patent leather shoes, and think it's a riot to stick chopsticks up my nose."

———

HE *WRITES*: "Had it with the singles' scene…?"

HE **MEANS**: "I've struck out in every bar in town."

· ·

HE *WRITES*: "Lots to love."

HE **MEANS**: "I'm a hippo."

HE *WRITES*: "Single father of three seeks family-oriented female with plenty of love for his brood."

HE **MEANS**: "My babysitter raised her fee to three bucks an hour so I shipped her back to Bora Bora."

....

HE *WRITES*: "Imaginative dreamer."

HE **MEANS**: "When the world catches on, I'm going to make a killing on toilet paper that lights up in the dark."

HE *WRITES*: "Part Tom Hanks, part Paul Reiser."

HE **MEANS**: "Mostly Gumby."

· ·

HE *WRITES*: "Complex, with subtle dark streak."

HE **MEANS**: "I'm on Prozac."

HE *WRITES*: "Seeks strong woman."

HE **MEANS**: "To haul out the garbage and re-side my house."

· ·

HE *WRITES*: "Thirty-something guy looking for twenty-something counterpart."

HE **MEANS**: "Fifty-something geezer looking for Lolita."

———

HE *WRITES*: "Motivated foreigner wishes to get acquainted with attractive American-born lady."

HE *MEANS*: "Who will sponsor me and finance a fruit and vegetable stand."

• •

HE *WRITES*: "Seeks beautiful spirit. Photo a **must**."

HE *MEANS*: "**Must** look like Cindy Crawford—even if you're Mother Teresa!"

HE *WRITES*: "Higher education."

HE **MEANS**: "The judge sent me to bad-driving school."

· ·

HE *WRITES*: "Wish to relocate to a special island with that special lady."

HE **MEANS**: "I'm in the witness protection program."

HE *WRITES*: "SWM seeks petite Oriental lady."

HE ***MEANS***: "Macho man seeks woman who will walk on my back—or three feet behind me."

HE *WRITES*: "Youthful appearance."

HE **MEANS**: "I have a lifetime membership in the Hair Club for Men."

. . . .

HE *WRITES*: "Seeks gal who's equally at home in lace and jeans."

HE **MEANS**: "Seeks gal who's great in the bedroom...and will clean up after."

HE *WRITES*: "Looking for healthy gal with a great heart."

HE ***MEANS***: "I need a transplant."

· ·

HE *WRITES*: "Still just a kid at heart."

HE ***MEANS***: "Still makes messes, dribbles, and throws tantrums."

Alien States: Fidelity, Commitment, and Marriage

HE *SAYS*:   "You're the only woman in my life."

HE *MEANS*: "You're the only broad I know I can score with!"

HE SAYS: "I don't have a problem with commitment."

HE **MEANS**:   "That's because I'll never make one."

· ·

HE SAYS: "You deserve someone better than me, honey."

HE **MEANS**:   "I've got someone better than **you** waiting in my convertible."

HE S<small>AYS</small>:   "Your friend Cynthia…? Yeah, I think I vaguely remember her."

HE *M<small>EANS</small>*:   "The 42-23-36 with the mole two inches above her left thigh."

. . . .

HE S<small>AYS</small>:   "Trust me. You won't be sorry."

HE *M<small>EANS</small>*:   "**I** won't be sorry!"

HE SAYS: "I need more space."

HE **MEANS**: "I need more space…for ten or twenty other women."

· ·

HE SAYS: "I swear I'll leave my wife right after my little boy's graduation."

HE **MEANS**: "From med school."

HE SAYS: "Of **course** I've been committed before!"

HE **MEANS**: "To prisons, drug programs, and psycho wards."

· ·

HE SAYS: "I was late because the bus broke down."

HE **MEANS**: "Three hours after I stopped off for a few with the guys."

HE SAYS: "You're right. So now I'll be
completely honest with you."

HE **MEANS**:   "Shoot! Only three seconds to come
up with a better lie."

HE SAYS: "My wife doesn't understand me."

HE **MEANS**: "My wife doesn't understand my need to pick up bimbos in bars."

· ·

HE SAYS: "I'll be home as soon as I finish this report, sweetheart."

HE **MEANS**: "I'll be home as soon as the bartender yells 'last call.'"

——

HE SAYS: "My wife and I are separated."

HE **MEANS**: "My wife is home in bed—and I'm here with YOU in bed."

. . . .

HE SAYS: "I believe in fidelity."

HE **MEANS**: "For my wife and all my mistresses."

HE SAYS: "Separate vacations will give us the chance to pursue our individual passions."

HE **MEANS**: "MINE are Lynda, Tammi, and Monica."

· ·

HE SAYS: "Let's do lunch on Tuesday at ten and avoid the crowds."

HE **MEANS**: "Like my wife, my neighbors, and my coworkers."

HE SAYS: "I am **not** having a midlife crisis."

HE *MEANS*: "I always chased bimbos!—I just couldn't afford the gold jewelry, the red Ferrari, and the hair transplant before now."

HE SAYS: "I'm totally against open marriages for couples."

HE **MEANS**: "Husbands, however, are a different story."

....

HE SAYS: "I hired Chloe because she's dynamite with figures."

HE **MEANS**: "44-26-36."

HE SAYS: "What do you mean you want to get out and 'find' yourself? There's nothing out there but a bunch of horny married bums cruising for action. Believe me, I know."

HE **MEANS**: "I'm one of them."

HE SAYS: "Every man should have a wife."

HE **MEANS**: "Someone else's."

....

HE SAYS: "But sweetie, how could I possibly leave you...?"

HE **MEANS**: "You haven't finished making the car payments yet."

HE SAYS: "I'm finally ready for marriage."

HE **MEANS**: "My mother won't iron my shirts any-more."
"My apartment's being condemned by the Board of Health."
"My accountant says it's cheaper."
"I've blown my credit card on 900 'Hot 'n' Horny' calls."
"My local McDonald's moved across town."

Dirty Domestic Tricks

HE SAYS: "I'd give you the shirt off my back, babe."

HE *MEANS*: "So you can wash and iron it."

HE SAYS: "I'll help with the dishes just as soon as I'm out of the bathroom, hon."

HE **MEANS**: "I'm shooting for next Christmas—or when Halley's comet returns."

· ·

HE SAYS: "But you're so much better with the kids, sweetheart."

HE **MEANS**: "YOU take care of it. The Superbowl's on."

———

HE SAYS: "I'm more than willing to do my share around here."

HE **MEANS**: "I'm more than willing to lift my feet so you can crawl under the sofa with the Dustbuster and roll over so you can make the bed."

....

HE SAYS: "You know you can always count on me."

HE **MEANS**: "Except during football, baseball, basketball, and hockey seasons."

HE SAYS: "I still think of you the same way I always did, darling."

HE **MEANS**: "My maid."

. . . .

HE SAYS: "I promise I'll finish the playroom in time for the holidays."

HE **MEANS**: "New Year's, 2001."

HE SAYS: "So how was your day, dear...?"

HE **MEANS**: "Did you remember to wash my clothes, clean the toilets, and replace the batteries in the remote control?"

· ·

HE SAYS: "Tonight, leave all the cooking to me, darling!"

HE **MEANS**: "Should I order your pizza with or without anchovies?"

HE SAYS:　　"I'll be glad to help with the groceries."

HE **MEANS**:　"I'll hold the door while you lug them in."

• •

HE SAYS:　　"I pride myself on being self-sufficient."

HE **MEANS**:　"Don't I get my own beer during halftime?"

HE SAYS: "Of COURSE I took care of it!"

HE **MEANS**:   "Now think…was it taking the dog to the vet, or taking her mother to the Emergency Room…?"

• •

HE SAYS: "I believe in simplifying."

HE **MEANS**:   "It's simpler for me to find my clothes on the floor than in the closet."

HE SAYS: "You need to get outdoors more, hon."

HE **MEANS**: "You need to mow the lawn and clean the pool."

• •

HE SAYS: "How 'bout I throw something on the barbecue tonight so you can take it easy."

HE **MEANS**: "How 'bout you shop, husk the corn, marinate the meat, and clean the grill—while I watch the game."

HE SAYS: "You'll make a wonderful mother."

HE **MEANS**: "Finally! A woman who will cook for me, pick up my dirty underwear, and pamper me when I'm sick…just like Mom used to!"

· ·

HE SAYS: "I'll be happy to help with the baby."

HE **MEANS**: "I'll be happy to tell you when he screams or needs a diaper change."

HE SAYS: "Darling, if you'll let me…I'll put you on a pedestal."

HE **MEANS**: "So you can clean the cobwebs and paint the ceiling."

Job Jive

HE SAYS: "I'm a free-lance consultant."

HE MEANS: "I haven't had a paycheck since the Hoover administration."

HE SAYS: "I have income from private sources."

HE **MEANS**: "Alimony, disability, and unemployment insurance."

· ·

HE SAYS: "I'm in communications."

HE **MEANS**: "I install cable boxes."

HE SAYS: "I work in the financial district."

HE **MEANS**: "I have a hot-dog stand on Wall Street."

• •

HE SAYS: "I'm into water conservation."

HE **MEANS**: "I fix leaky toilets."

HE SAYS: "I'm in the film biz."

HE **MEANS**: "I'm a ticket-taker at the XXX Triplex on 42nd Street."

• •

HE SAYS: "I'm involved with the courts."

HE **MEANS**: "I'm on parole."

HE SAYS: "I'm in politics."

HE **MEANS**: "I'm on parole."

. . . .

HE SAYS: "I'm in hotel management."

HE **MEANS**: "I'm a bellhop."

HE SAYS: "I'm just waiting tables part-time between acting jobs."

HE **MEANS**: "I haven't had a role since I played the horn on _My Mother the Car._"

· ·

HE SAYS: "I'm an entrepreneur in the tropics."

HE **MEANS**: "I own a pineapple stand in Maui."

HE SAYS: "I'm in high-volume auto road service."

HE **MEANS**: "I squirt people's windshields on the parkway."

. . . .

HE SAYS: "I manage beachfront property."

HE **MEANS**: "I run a salt-water taffy concession in Atlantic City."

HE SAYS: "I'm in commodities."

HE **MEANS**: "I deliver eggs."

· ·

HE SAYS: "I direct."

HE **MEANS**: "I'm a traffic cop."

HE SAYS: "I'm in ladies' wear."

HE **MEANS**: "I'm a transvestite."

. . . .

HE SAYS: "I'm a gold speculator."

HE **MEANS**: "I hang around the beach with a metal detector."

HE SAYS: "I've been given keys to the executive washroom."

HE **MEANS**: "I clean the latrines at IBM."

. . . .

HE SAYS: "I'm an oil man."

HE **MEANS**: "I pump gas."

HE SAYS: "I'm into recycling."

HE **MEANS**: "I'm a garbage man."

· ·

HE SAYS: "I work in late-night television."

HE **MEANS**: "I'm the night watchman at *Letterman*."

———

HE S<small>AYS</small>: "I live off an annual trust."

HE **M<small>EANS</small>**: "My mom sends me a hundred bucks on my birthday."

Mucho Macho: **<u>Real</u>** Women Make Quiche!

HE SAYS: "I agree a relationship should be fifty-fifty."

HE **MEANS**: "You give fifty, I take fifty."

HE SAYS: "Of course it doesn't bother me that you make more money than me."

HE MEANS: "Of course don't ever expect me to get it up with you again."

HE SAYS: "There you go! Being irrational!"

HE **MEANS**: "There you go! Disagreeing with me!"

· ·

HE SAYS: "You're a fascinating conversationalist."

HE **MEANS**: "You listen while I do all the talking."

HE SAYS: "A woman can be attractive at any age."

HE **MEANS**: "Under thirty. After that, she's over the hill."

· ·

HE SAYS: "I believe communication is a two-way street."

HE **MEANS**: "I talk; you listen."

HE SAYS: "Of course I don't mind if you get a job, dear."

HE **MEANS**: "As long as it doesn't interfere with your cooking my meals, washing my clothes, scrubbing my floors—and being my sex slave."

· ·

HE SAYS: "We've both learned something from that argument."

HE **MEANS**: "That I was right!"

HE SAYS: "Each of us should have an equal say around here."

HE **MEANS**: "I'll tell you how we'll spend our money and where we'll live; you'll tell me whether we should go with the dark blue or aqua toilet paper."

HE SAYS: "Of course it's normal for you to disagree with me now and then."

HE **MEANS**: "It's that PMS again, right...?"

· ·

HE SAYS: "We're equal partners in this marriage."

HE **MEANS**: "YOU be the silent one."

HE SAYS: "Fair is fair. I think you **should** go out one night a week with the girls."

HE **MEANS**: "And so should I!"

· ·

HE SAYS: "I agree all decisions should be discussed."

HE **MEANS**: "I decide, **then** we discuss…what I decided."

HE SAYS: "I hate the fact that we've lowered the standards in this country."

HE **MEANS**: "The **double** standard."

....

HE SAYS: "I'm all for the women's movement."

HE **MEANS**: "I'm all for women moving my dirty clothes from the floor to the washer to the dryer."

HE SAYS: "All this pre-nupt does is spell out fairly what's mine."

HE **MEANS**:   "The house, the furniture, the stocks, and your income."

• •

HE SAYS: "I'm a big supporter of women in the marketplace."

HE **MEANS**:   "Sara Lee, Betty Crocker, and Aunt Jemima."

The Dim, the Dumb, and the Dishonest

HE SAYS: "Why ask directions?! I know where we are!"

HE MEANS: "Somewhere between the Okefenokees and the Bermuda Triangle."

HE SAYS: "Obviously, there's something wrong with this VCR!"

HE **MEANS**: "No matter how many times I bang it, the flashing light still won't go off!"

· ·

HE SAYS: "I promise I'll start my diet as soon as I pick up some Sweet & Low at the store tomorrow."

HE **MEANS**: "And a month's supply of Raisinets and Ding Dongs I can hide in the garage tonight."

HE SAYS: "Don't worry! I bought enough hors d'oeuvres for an army."

HE **MEANS**:   "Three bags of Fritos and a can of beer nuts."

· ·

HE SAYS: (In a fire) "You grab the kids! I'll grab our vital possessions."

HE **MEANS**:   "My high school beer mug, my *Big Mamma* annuals, and my polyester Nehru jacket."

HE SAYS: (Moaning) "Make me fresh orange juice and chicken soup, fluff up my pillows, bring me a heating pad, and call to make sure the will's in order."

HE MEANS: "I've got a head cold."

· ·

HE SAYS: "I am perfectly capable of having a meaningful discussion."

HE MEANS: "As long as it's about baseball, bimbos, and beer."

HE SAYS: "I prefer TV shows that raise thought-provoking questions."

HE **MEANS**: "I wonder if those *Baywatch* babes ever had a boob job?"

· ·

HE SAYS: "I'm into memorabilia."

HE **MEANS**: "I saved my tenth-grade *National Geographic* 'native' issues."

HE SAYS: "I do a lot of spiritual reading."

HE **MEANS**: "I read my fortune before wolfing down the cookies at Mei Fong's."

• •

HE SAYS: "I'm often plagued by deep questions."

HE **MEANS**: "Like how Vanna White can be a babe AND hold down such a tough job."

HE SAYS: "I can't live without you."

HE **MEANS**: "I can't work the Mr. Coffee without you."

. . . .

HE SAYS: "I've learned the art of conversation from the masters."

HE **MEANS**: "Beavis and Butt-Head."

HE SAYS: "You're nuts! My waist is still thirty-three inches. I measured myself just yesterday!"

HE **MEANS**: "Around the knees."

· ·

HE SAYS: "That's my beeper. Sorry babe, but it's important."

HE **MEANS**: "It's my mother...to tell me she finished my laundry."

HE SAYS: "You're such a perfectionist!"

HE **MEANS**: "It's only a small burn in your mother's coffee table."

....

HE SAYS: "I never lie."

HE **MEANS**: "I omit."

HE SAYS: "There you go again, jumping to conclusions."

HE **MEANS**:   "Just because you found me naked in a hotel room with a cheerleader doesn't **prove** anything actually happened."

HE SAYS: "I admit it, it's all my fault."

HE **MEANS**: "For being dumb enough to get caught."

· ·

HE SAYS: "I love horses."

HE **MEANS**: "I **play** the horses."

HE SAYS: "I need a cellular phone—for emergencies."

HE **MEANS**: "And to impress the cashier at K mart and the bimbo at the car wash."

HE SAYS: "I often go on exotic vacations."

HE **MEANS**: "I often check out the action in Tijuana."

· ·

HE SAYS: "I always try to stay in control."

HE **MEANS**: "Rent control, birth control, remote control."

HE SAYS: "I swear I'll never do that again."

HE **MEANS**: "Except when I forget, or **feel** like doing it again."

"Boys Will Be Boys"

HE SAYS: "Hey babe...a man's gotta do what a man's gotta do."

HE MEANS: "Break wind, spit, and scratch his crotch."

HE SAYS: "I'm just naturally musical."

HE **MEANS**:   "I can whistle 'A Hundred Bottles of Beer on the Wall' with my mouth shut."

· ·

HE SAYS: "I'm very coordinated."

HE **MEANS**:   "I manage to pee within three inches of the toilet bowl."

HE SAYS: "I make it a point to practice water conservation."

HE MEANS: "I make it a point to shower and wash my underwear only once a month."

HE SAYS: "I'm never grumpy in the morning."

HE **MEANS**: "I sleep till noon."

· ·

HE SAYS: "What do you mean I don't have good table manners...?"

HE **MEANS**: "Don't I always wait to belch till **after** the main course?"

HE SAYS: "I'll stand up for anything!"

HE **MEANS**: "Except an elderly or pregnant woman on a bus."

• •

HE SAYS: "I'm into gourmet food."

HE **MEANS**: "Brochette of Spam with French's mustard."

HE SAYS: "A smart look is never out of style."

HE **MEANS**: "Polyester leisure suits and white socks."

· ·

HE SAYS: "You wouldn't understand. It's a 'man' thing."

HE **MEANS**: "Mooning strangers, challenging your pals to a game of knucks when you're loaded, and blowing straw wrappers at IHOP is too hip for a mere female to appreciate."

HE SAYS: "I'm a meticulous dresser."

HE **MEANS**: "My socks match."

· ·

HE SAYS: "I've never had a mid-life crisis."

HE **MEANS**: "I've never left puberty."

Quickie Manspeak Lies

*The following are statements "he" makes that are **never** true. They've been handed down through generations, and some experts feel they are instinctive.*

"I'm looking through the *Victoria's Secret* catalog for you, dear."

"Why do I save them…? Don't you realize those stacks of *Playboys* will be worth a fortune some day!"

"Funny, this is **my** first time in this bar, too."

"I'm leaving my wife as soon as she has that operation."

————————————

"Of course I'm interested in your feelings."

————————————

"I'll be thinking about you every minute during the convention."

"Of course I'll call you after Labor Day, when we're back in the city."

———————————

"I'll have that fixed (or put together) in a jiffy."

———————————

"Vegas just wasn't any fun without you."

———

"Me…? No way! She must be confusing me with someone else!"

———————

"You've been getting hang-ups and wrong numbers? Search me! Ever since the phone company broke up, you just can't trust 'em."

———————

"Believe me, I feel as lousy about what I did as you do."

"I think your stretch marks are beautiful. They show you've lived."

———————————

(When suggesting an affair) "I want you to know...I've never done this before."

———————————

"I treat your mother exactly the same way I treat mine."

———————————

"I swear, babe, I haven't touched my wife in MONTHS."

———————————————

"I'll marry you as soon as my play is finished."

———————————————

"I promise to love, honor, and obey."

...And Yes, They Manspeak to Each Other Too! A Sampling of Bar-Buddy Bull

HE SAYS: "Nah! Hey...she wasn't my type anyway."

HE MEANS: "She dumped me."

HE SAYS: "Hey, pal, you're better off. Frankly, she was no prize."

HE **MEANS**: "By the way…what's her number?"

HE S AYS: "Our sex life is fast and furious, man."

HE **MEANS**:   "I was fast and she was furious."

· ·

HE S AYS: "Hey…you know broads. They play hard to get."

HE **MEANS**:   "She got an order of protection."

HE SAYS: "It's the wife who's into soaps, pal.
I don't watch that crap!"

HE **MEANS**: "I'm into *Baywatch* and reruns of
Gilligan's Island."

....

HE SAYS: "Me…? I make in the six figures."

HE **MEANS**: "If you count cents."

HE SAYS: "I can 'go' all night."

HE **MEANS**: "I have a prostate problem."

· ·

HE SAYS: "Tell me! I was in uniform for four years."

HE **MEANS**: "The Cub Scouts."

HE SAYS: "Whaddya mean? My weight hasn't changed in twenty years!"

HE MEANS: "I've just shrunk three inches."

And Finally...
The Manspeak-eth the Truth

HE *SAYS*:   "I'm really not very complicated."

HE ***MEANS***: "I'm really not very complicated."

ABOUT THE AUTHOR

Marnie Winston-Macauley, a.k.a. "Cyber-Sadie" on-line, is a writer, therapist, and advice columnist. In addition to *Manspeak: What He Says...What He Really Means*, she is the author of *The Ultimate Sex, Love & Romance Quiz Book, The Ultimate Sex, Love & Romance Quiz Book II, Men We Love to Hate: The Book*, and its companion calendar, *Men We Love to Hate 1997 Calendar*, and co-author of *He Says/She Says*, all of which are also published by Andrews and McMeel. Ms. Winston-Macauley, as Cyber-Sadie, is the advice mavin–plus on ABC Love Online (America Online), and offers up her wit and wisdom on America Online's Entertainment Channel twice weekly. Her quizzes have appeared on ABC Love Online and HomeArts, Hearst's on-line network. In addition, she has written hundreds of articles for magazines and newspapers around the world, and was a writer for the daytime drama *As the World Turns*. Her scripts were chosen for submission to the Emmy Blue Ribbon panel following the Best Writing nomination and for the Writer's Guild Award. Her other fiction works include science fiction novelettes for *The Magazine of Fantasy & Science Fiction* and *Realms of Fantasy*. Ms. Winston-Macauley has been a guest on hundreds of radio and television shows, including, among others, *Charles Perez, The Mark Walberg Show, USA LIVE*, and *Mike & Maty*.